Donald's Feelings

by Liza Charlesworth

No part of this publication may be reproduced, stored in a retrieval system, or transmitted in any form or by any means, electronic, mechanical, photocopying, recording, or otherwise, without written permission of the publisher. For information regarding permission, write to Scholastic Inc., Attention: Permissions Department, 557 Broadway, New York, NY 10012.

ISBN 978-1-338-13072-0

Copyright © 2018 Disney Enterprises, Inc. All rights reserved.

All rights reserved. Published by Scholastic Inc., *Publishers since 1920*. SCHOLASTIC and associated logos are trademarks and/or registered trademarks of Scholastic Inc.

10 9 8 7 6 5 4 3 2 1   18 19 20 21 22
Printed in the U.S.A.   40
First printing, February 2018

SCHOLASTIC INC.

Donald is happy.

Donald is sad.

Donald is scared.

Donald is hungry.

Donald is mad.

Donald is bored.

Donald is excited.

Donald is tired.

Donald is surprised.

Donald is very happy!

Comprehension Boosters

1. On page 3, why is Donald sad?

2. On page 15, why is Donald very happy?

3. What feelings have you had today? Talk about them.